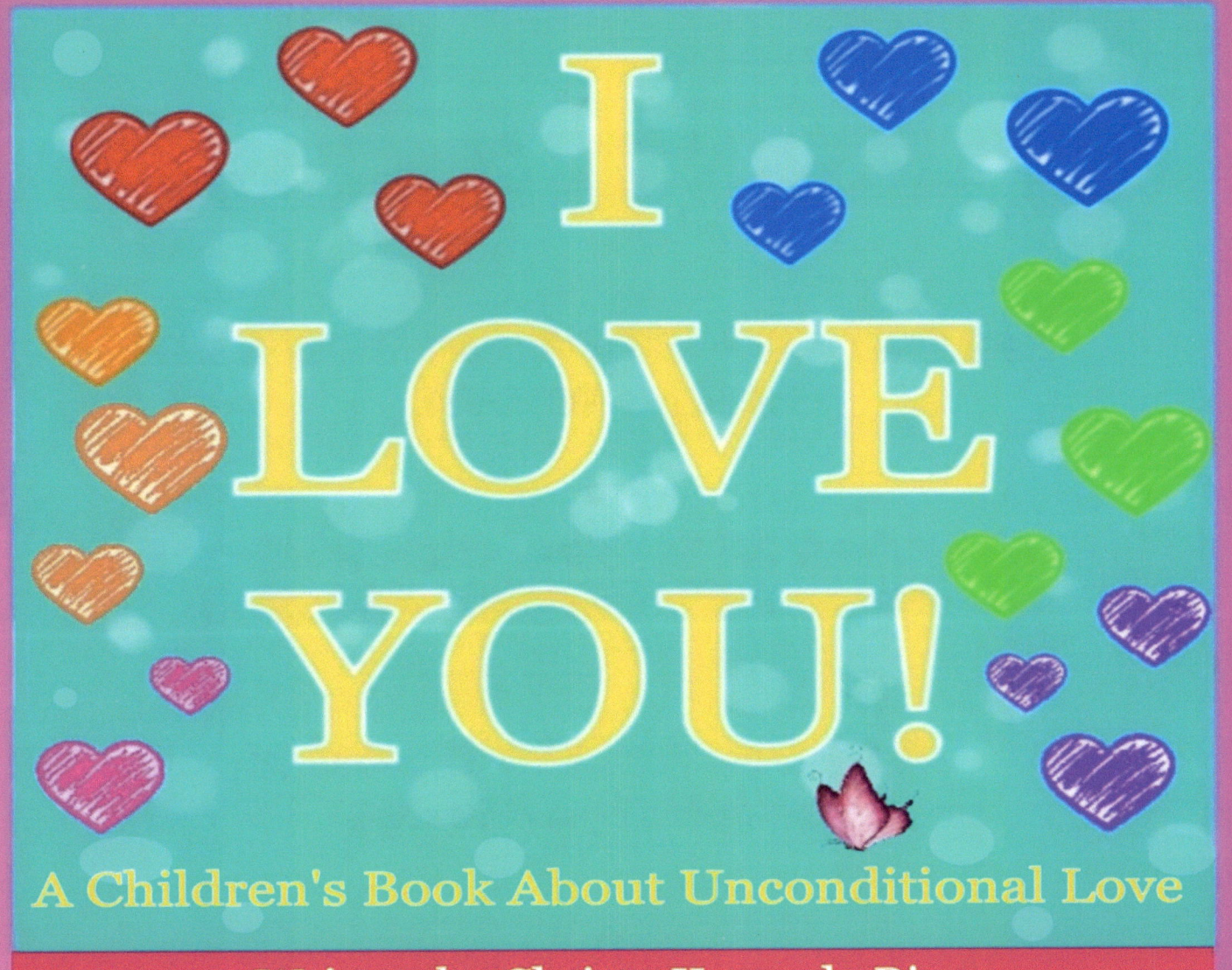

I LOVE YOU!
A Children's Book About Unconditional Love

Text Copyright - 2025 Christy Kennedy Rice
All rights reserved.

Paperback ISBN 979-8-218-29418-2
Hardcover ISBN 979-8-218-34473-3

All inquiries should be directed to
www.kennedysisters.com

Kennedy Sisters

Casey and Rachel,
My favorite place is with you.
Love, Mom

This book is dedicated to the children and young adults in my family.

Casey, Rachel, Blu, Bradyn, Lucas, Madie, Jack, Ellie, Sam, Adelaide, Hadleigh, Aliza, Briggs, Michael, Isaac, Amelia, Violet, Scarlett, Ivy, Jordan, Caroline, Major, McKayla, Katelyn, Wyatt, Ellie Kate, & Austin

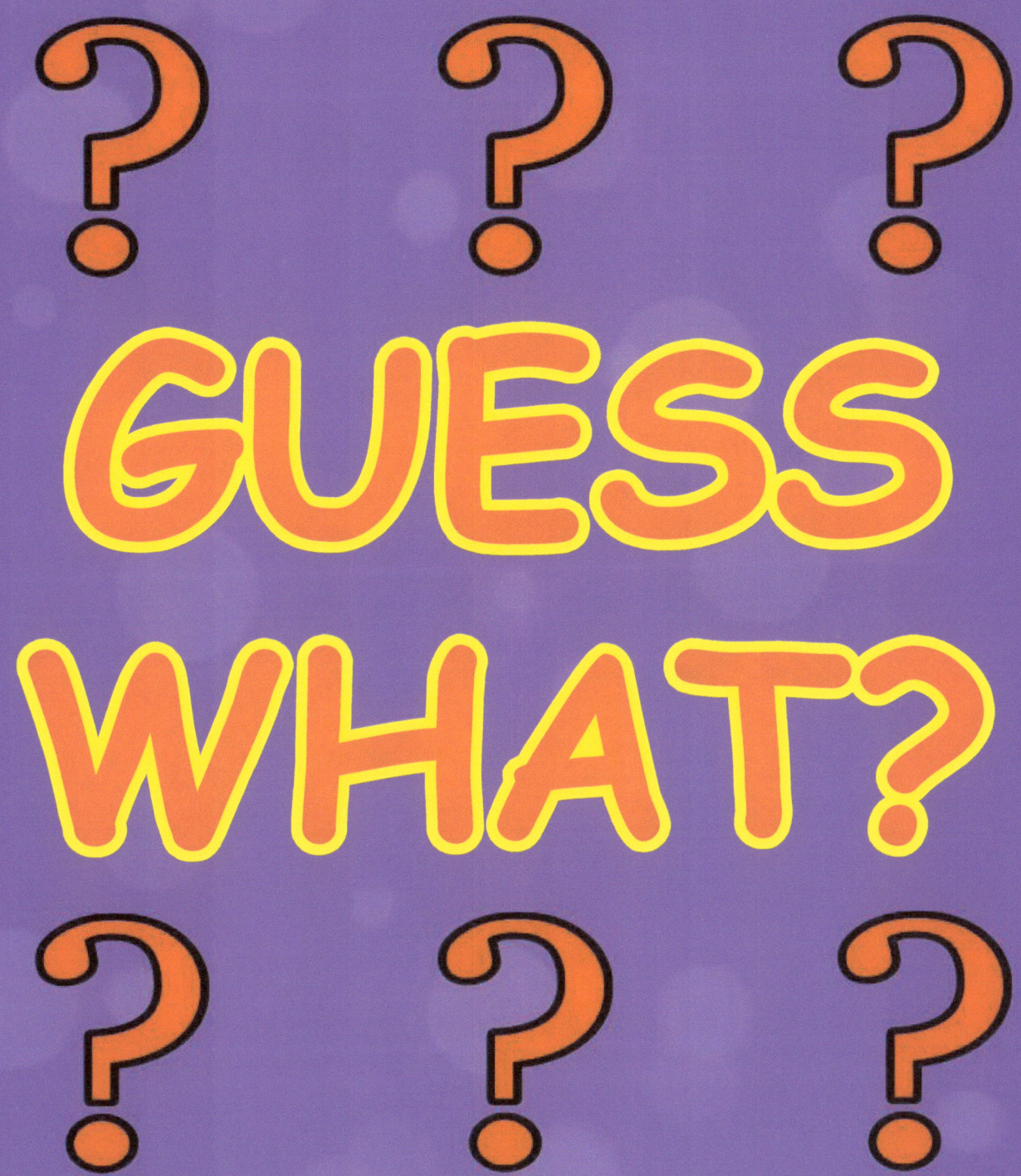

I loved you yesterday. I love you today. I will love you tomorrow. I love you always.

Yesterday =

Today =

Tomorrow =

I love you on Sundays, Mondays, Tuesdays, Wednesdays, Thursdays, Fridays, and Saturdays.

I love you in January, February, March, April, May, June, July, August, September, October, November, and December.

I love you this year. I loved you last year. I will love you next year. I love you every year.

2001	2011	2021	2031	2041
2002	2012	2022	2032	2042
2003	2013	2023	2033	2043
2004	2014	2024	2034	2044
2005	2015	2025	2035	2045
2006	2016	2026	2036	2046
2007	2017	2027	2037	2047
2008	2018	2028	2038	2048
2009	2019	2029	2039	2049
2010	2020	2030	2040	2050

I love you in spring, summer, fall, and winter.

I love you on sunny days, rainy days, and snowy days.

I love you all through the night when the sky is dark.

I love you in the morning when the sky is bright.

I love you when you are sick.
I love you when you are well.

I love you when you make the best choices. I love you when you make mistakes.

Best Choices

Mistakes

? ? ? ? ?

Decisions

? ? ? ? ?

I love you when you are happy.
I love you when you are sad.

I love you when you play. I love you when you rest.

I will love you when you earn 1st place. I will love you when you earn 2nd, 3rd, 4th, and 5th place.

I will love you when you earn last place too. I love you when you win and when you lose.

I love you when you are dirty.

I love you when you are quiet. I love you when you are loud.

I love you when you sleep. I love you when you are awake.

I am proud of you and very thankful you are in my life.

I AM PROUD OF YOU!

I AM THANKFUL FOR YOU!

I LOVE YOU!

These pages are for you.
Write the names of the people you love the most.

www.ingramcontent.com/pod-product-compliance
Lightning Source LLC
Chambersburg PA
CBHW041151060526
44107CB00142B/1179